GETTING TO KNOW THE WORLD'S GREATEST ARTISTS

E D W A R D
HOPPER

WRITTEN AND ILLUSTRATED BY MIKE VENEZIA

CONSULTANT SARA MOLLMAN UNDERHILL

CP CHILDRENS PRESS®

CHICAGO

For my friends at Childrens Press,
especially Fran and Grit

Cover: *Nighthawks*. 1942. Oil on canvas, 30 x 57 inches.
   Friends of American Art Collection.
   Photograph © 1990 The Art Institute of Chicago.
   All Rights Reserved

Library of Congress Cataloging-in-Publication Data

Venezia, Mike.
  Edward Hopper / written and illustrated by Mike
Venezia.
      p.   cm. — (Getting to know the world's greatest
artists)
  Summary: Briefly examines the life and work of the
American realist painter, describing and giving examples
of his art.
  ISBN 0-516-02277-6
  1. Hopper, Edward, 1882-1967—Juvenile literature.
2. Painters—United States—Biography—Juvenile
literature. [1. Hopper, Edward, 1882-1967.
2. Artists. 3. Painting, American. 4. Painting,
Modern—United States. 5. Art appreciation.]
I. Title. II. Series.
ND237.H75V46   1989
759.13—dc20   90-2166
[B]   CIP
[92]   AC

Self Portrait. 1925-1930. Oil on canvas, 25 1/16 x 20 3/8 inches.
Collection of Whitney Museum of American Art. Josephine N. Hopper Bequest

Edward Hopper was born in
Nyack, New York, in 1882. He was
one of America's greatest artists, and
was known as an American realist
painter.

Manhattan Bridge Loop. 1928. Oil on canvas, 35 x 60 inches.
Addison Gallery of Art, Phillips Academy, Andover, Massachusetts. Gift of Stephen C. Clark

Even if you've never seen Edward Hopper's paintings before, many of them might look familiar to you. That's because he painted pictures of real, everyday things.

Pennsylvania Coal Town. 1947. Oil on canvas, 28 x 40 inches.
The Butler Institute of American Art, Youngstown, Ohio

Hopper painted the people and
places you might see from the
window of a car as you drive through
different cities and neighborhoods.

Edward Hopper always liked to
draw. When he was very young, he
got a blackboard as a gift.

His mother encouraged Edward
and his sister, Marion, to draw. It was
one of their favorite things to do.

Edward Hopper
lived right next to
the Hudson River
while he was growing
up. He saw all kinds
of boats coming and
going, and even built
his own small sailboat
when he was 14.
Hopper always loved
water and boats, and he
painted many pictures
of them.

The Long Leg. 1935. Oil on canvas, 20 x 30¼ inches.
The Virginia Steele Scott Collection. Henry E. Huntington Library and Art Gallery

When Edward Hopper was 12 years old, he grew very quickly to be 6 feet tall! He may have felt funny about being so much taller than other kids his age, because he started to spend a lot of time alone.

(Hook Mountain, Nyack). c. 1899.
Watercolor on paper, 5 x 7 inches.
Collection of Whitney Museum
of American Art. Josephine N.
Hopper Bequest

COLUMBIA

Columbia. c. 1896-1898. Ink on paper, 8 x 5 inches.
Collection of Whitney Museum of American Art.
Josephine N. Hopper Bequest

Sketch of a Dog. June 12, 1893.
Pencil on paper, 15 x 11 inches.
Collection of Whitney Museum of American Art.
Josephine N. Hopper Bequest

Below: (Steam Engine; Railroad of New Jersey). c. 1896.
Pencil on paper, 8 x 10 inches. Collection of Whitney
Museum of American Art. Josephine N. Hopper Bequest

Edward stayed in his room a lot.
He spent his time reading and
drawing pictures like the ones shown
above.

Edward Hopper's parents knew how much he wanted to be an artist. After he graduated from high school, they sent him to New York City to study art.

In New York, Hopper learned from a great teacher, Robert Henri. Henri taught his students to look around them and see life as it really was. Henri believed there was beauty and lots of interesting things to see in the city.

Henri said that slum buildings, and the people who lived in them, and

even factories with smokestacks, could be beautiful. Hopper liked Henri's ideas. Most other artists of the time would never dream of painting these things.

After he left art school, Hopper
made three trips to Paris, France,
where he studied painting on his
own. Edward Hopper saw all the
supermodern art that was being done
in Paris, but it didn't impress him
very much.

Paris Street. 1906. Oil on wood, 13 x 9⅜ inches.
Collection of Whitney Museum of American Art.
Josephine N. Hopper Bequest

Stairway at 48 rue de Lille, Paris. 1906.
Oil on wood, 13 x 9¼ inches.
Collection of Whitney Museum of American Art.
Josephine N. Hopper Bequest

He was still interested in painting real, everyday things. After his third trip to Paris, he went back to New York and took a job as an illustrator, drawing pictures for magazines and ads.

Hopper didn't like his job very much, because his bosses were always telling him how to do his illustrations. The only reason he kept on doing them was to make money.

Cover of
*Hotel/Motel
Management,*
November 1924

Hopper's illustrations were pretty
good, even if he didn't like doing
them.

Sailing. c. 1911. Oil on canvas, 24 x 29 inches. The Carnegie Museum of Art, Pittsburgh.
Gift of Mr. and Mrs. James H. Beal in honor of the Sarah Scaife Gallery, 1972

During his time off, Hopper kept painting. He sold his first painting at a famous art exhibition in New York called the Armory Show. He named the painting *Sailing,* and got $250 for it!

Night in the Park. 1921. Etching, 13⅜ x 16 inches.
Philadelphia Museum of Art, purchased: The Harrison Fund

Hopper didn't have much luck after the Armory Show. He couldn't sell any of his paintings or even get anyone interested in them for a long time. He thought he would try a different kind of art for a while. He decided to do etchings, a type of printing done on metal plates.

Night Shadows. 1921. Etching, 12³⁄₁₆ x 15¹⁵⁄₁₆ inches.
Collection of Whitney Museum of Art. Josephine N. Hopper Bequest

Hopper learned a lot about light, shadows, and choice of subjects from making etchings. People liked Hopper's etchings. He won prizes for his work and he started to become well known.

House by the Railroad. 1925. Oil on canvas, 24 x 29 inches.
Collection, The Museum of Modern Art, New York. Given Anonymously.

For ten years, Hopper hardly painted at all. But since his etchings were popular, he thought it might be a good time to start painting again. Soon he was making watercolors and oil paintings.

Lighthouse Hill. 1927. Oil on canvas, 28¼ x 39½ inches.
Dallas Museum of Art. Gift of Mr. and Mrs. Maurice Purnell

Hopper's paintings finally started selling. He was able to leave his illustrating job, and he decided to marry a girl he met in art school. Her name was Jo Nivison. Jo admired Hopper's work and she always encouraged him. She was an artist, too.

New York Movie. 1939. Oil on canvas, 32¼ x 40⅛ inches.
Collection, The Museum of Modern Art, New York. Given Anonymously.

Hopper used Jo as a model in practically every painting he did that had a woman in it. Sometimes he changed the color of her hair or put her in different costumes.

The Hoppers never had children.
They lived a very plain life and didn't
like to spend money on fancy food,
clothes, or cars. They did enjoy

Gas. 1940. Oil on canvas, 26¼ x 40¼ inches. Collection,
The Museum of Modern Art, New York. Mrs. Simon Guggenheim Fund.

driving around the country, though,
stopping to paint scenes of America
that caught Edward Hopper's eye.

New York Office. 1962. Oil on canvas, 40 x 55 inches. Collection of the
Montgomery Museum of Fine Arts, Montgomery, Alabama. The Blount Collection

Hopper used strong shapes,
shadows, and lighting to make
everyday things interesting.

Sometimes it's fun to guess what
the people in Hopper's paintings are
doing or thinking about.

Hotel Room. 1931. Oil on canvas, 60 x 65 inches.
Thyssen-Bornemisza Collection, Lugano, Switzerland

Is the lady in the hotel room
reading an important letter, or is she
just checking her hotel bill? Do you
think she'll be staying in the hotel for
a long time, or just overnight? And
why does she look so serious?

Nighthawks. 1942. Oil on canvas, 30 x 57 inches. Friends of American Art Collection.
Photograph © 1990 The Art Institute of Chicago. All Rights Reserved

When you look at *Nighthawks,* you might wonder what the people are doing out so late at night. Although the restaurant is bright and warm, nobody looks very friendly or happy. The dark shadows and shapes of the buildings give you the feeling that something mysterious could happen at any moment.

Early Sunday Morning. 1930. Oil on canvas, 35 x 60 inches.
Collection of Whitney Museum of American Art, purchased
with funds from Gertrude Vanderbilt Whitney

Even without people in them,
Hopper's paintings of houses and
buildings make you wonder what
could be going on inside them.

Edward Hopper painted the ordinary things he saw in America, and made them special.

Manhattan Bridge Loop. 1928. Oil on canvas, 35 x 60 inches. Addison Gallery of Art, Phillips Academy, Andover, Massachusetts. Gift of Stephen C. Clark

He loved the way sunlight looked when it was shining on the side of a house, or the way a lamp lighted the inside of a room.

Second Story Sunlight. 1960. Oil on canvas, 40 x 50 inches. Collection of Whitney Museum of American Art, purchased with funds from the Friends of the Whitney Museum of American Art

His strong, solid shapes and shadows sometimes give you a feeling of mystery or loneliness.

Dawn in Pennsylvania. 1942. Oil on canvas, 24½ x 44¼ inches. © Daniel J. Terra Collection. Terra Museum of American Art, Chicago

Edward Hopper lived to be 85 years old. His unusual view of America makes him one of the greatest American artists.

Tables for Ladies. 1930. Oil on canvas, 48¼ x 60¼ inches. The Metropolitan Museum of Art. George A. Hearn Fund, 1931

The Hopper paintings in this book are in the museums listed below. If none of these museums are close to you, maybe you can visit one when you are on vacation.

Addison Gallery of Art, Andover, Massachusetts
The Art Institute of Chicago
The Butler Institute of American Art, Youngstown, Ohio
The Carnegie Museum of Art, Pittsburgh
Dallas Museum of Art
Henry E. Huntington Library and Art Gallery, San Marino, California
The Metropolitan Museum of Art, New York
Montgomery Museum of Fine Arts, Montgomery, Alabama
The Museum of Modern Art, New York
Philadelphia Museum of Art
Terra Museum of American Art, Chicago
Thyssen-Bornemisza Collection, Lugano, Switzerland
Whitney Museum of American Art, New York